"God Ain't Worth a Dime?"

Dr. Charles K. Williams

CONTENTS

ACKNOWLEDGMENTS

I like to thank my church the Standard of Living Ministries for all your prayers and support over the years. I'd like to thank Rachel Brown who transcribed this teaching from CD to Computer and paper. If it wasn't for you this probably wouldn't have gotten done. Last but not least, I would like to thank my family. Cynthia thank you for all of your love, encouragement, prayers and patients over the years as I prepared this lesson and others. Also to my lovely daughters Chanel and Charnae for your care, concern and prayers.

Chapter 1

The Tithe: The Dime that Sanctifies

There have been many books written that talk about tithing. But this book, with its controversial title, looks at tithing from a very simplistic and matter of fact point of view.

The title "God Ain't Worth a Dime" speaks volumes about how much we really value and trust God when it comes to our finances. This book title isn't only a statement it's a question. When someone tells you that you aren't worth a dime, what they are telling you is that ***you're worth very little or you're not worth redeeming.*** Conversely, in order for someone to come to that conclusion or make that statement they had to ask themselves that statement in a question form. Then after asking that question they had to come to that conclusion. Yep, you're not worth a dime, you're not worth redemption. We're not redeeming God with the dime or for that matter redeeming our souls as far as salvation is concerned. The dime is about the redemption of our finances/wellbeing. This is an observation I'd like to share with you regarding this financial redemption. **Unger's Bible Dictionary** says redemption in *Hebrew* means to deliver; to sever. In the *Greek* it means a loosing away; to buy, paying a price. Why is this significant? Silver in the bible speaks of redemption (Amos 8:6; Zechariah 11:12-13).

> **6 That we may _buy the poor for silver_,**
> **And the needy for a pair of sandals—**
> **Even sell the bad wheat?"**
>
> **Amos 8:6 (NKJV)**

Silver was used as a means of redeeming the poor from poverty. Your silver has that same power to redeem you from poverty today. The first dimes ever minted in the USA were made of silver. See the connection? So when you tithe you're freeing the rest of your money from the enemy's grip. Your silver (dime) sanctifies the rest of the money you have left. The dime, the smallest physical coin we carry, packs a lot of power and that's all God is asking for. **Think about this: when you release those dimes you're redeeming the rest of the money so it will go further, longer, and do more things.** Don't cheat yourself; it's not worth losing the effects of what that dime(s) would produce.

One dime out of every dollar is what you **owe** God. Yes, *owe* Him. It is God that gives you the power or ability to get wealth, so He already owns it all.

> **"And you shall remember the LORD your God, for [it is] He who gives you power to get wealth, that He may establish His covenant which He swore to your fathers, as [it is] this day.**
>
> **Deuteronomy 8:18**

3

Now that's quite a deal for God to even allow you to keep ninety percent of what's already His and only ask you for ten percent back. That's an excellent deal.

The tithe is the tenth or ten percent. Ten represents the whole. One tenth represents the whole. Like the Ten Commandments it represents all the laws of God. *If you can keep all ten, it's as good as you keeping all the laws.* Can anyone keep all ten other than Jesus? NO The book of James says, when you break one you're guilty of breaking them all **(James 2:10)**. Do you see how important the tithe, the tenth and the dime is? It represents the whole. Simply put, for every dollar that you receive you are supposed to give God a dime, ten percent, the tithe from it. If you receive $10.00 you owe God ten dimes. It's as simple as that. No one can go before God or the judgment seat and say that they didn't know how to tithe. I'm not saying that you'll have to go before the judgment seat for not tithing, but I'm just saying. I know that statement might rattle some religious cages - but don't be alarmed I'm not going to mess with you.

I have some questions to ask you. Why have you been holding out on giving God the dime? Is it because you don't trust Him? Why is that? If you don't have answers to those questions, take some time and think about it. But in the meantime, do you know every time you don't tithe, you

tell God – *God You Ain't worth a dime*. More people than would like to acknowledge tell God that He's not worth a dime.

Let me present this to you. How many of you, if you knew I had a dime would come and rob me for it. You wouldn't, right? It wouldn't even be worth your time. It

wouldn't be worth the time that you would spend in jail for

brandishing a weapon to rob me of the said dime. Honestly, you should get locked up if you robbed someone for a dime.

Do people really rob God for a dime? Let's see what Malachi says,

> **"Will a man rob God? Yet you have robbed Me! But you say, 'In what way have we robbed You?' In <u>tithes</u> (dimes) and offerings."**
>
> **Malachi 3:8**

So we see that a man will rob God for a dime(s). Yes indeed! He will stick God up in a minute. Every single Sunday people rob God for a dime of a dollar by not tithing. That's terrible. Sometimes when people are in the wrong they get selective amnesia. You say, how did I rob God? He answers, in tithes and offerings.

You *rob* God – you don't steal from God. Sometimes we say you steal from God. But the Bible emphatically states you <u>**rob**</u> God. When you rob someone that means that the person has knowledge of it. You're in their face. However, when you steal from someone they don't necessarily have to know that you're stealing from them. So a lot of people think they're just stealing from God when in fact they just stuck Him up for a dime(s).

People don't realize that when you don't give God an offering you're still robbing Him. That's how you stay poor.

Poor is an acronym. It means **Pass Over Offerings Regularly**. When you do that, you're robbing Him of the opportunity to increase **(i.e. manifest the blessing) (Luke 6:38)**, and to protect you. We'll get into that later. Increase can't come into your life like you or God want it to because you're hindering its flow when you don't give like you're supposed to. And when do that, you're putting yourself under a curse. In this economy you don't need the devil to have open access to you.

Jesus taught a parable in Matthew chapter 25 about three men who were given specific amounts of money. I'll

7

talk about this parable in detail later in the book. Bad things happened to the person who had the one talent because he didn't do what he was supposed to do with the money. I'm not just saying that there were negative consequences; Jesus said it.

Negative effects are linked to you in the area of your finances when you don't do what you're supposed to. It's like putting your money in a bag full of holes. It's like having someone sift your money. Giving God a dime of a dollar isn't hard to do. It's really not. You've got to be cheap or stupid not to give God the dime. I'm not trying to insult you, I'm only trying to wake you up by shaking you.

When I teach on tithing usually I ask the people in the meetings for a dime, most of them go into their pockets and or purses immediately and pull one out. They were eager and willing to give me the dime. Why? Because it's not a lot I'm asking for. Now, if I had asked them for $100 they probably would've thought I was out of my mind. However, the willingness that they had in giving me the dime is the same willingness that you should have towards giving it to God. If we look at it as simply as that – that we are just giving God a dime as opposed to giving him several dollars- it will be easier to give. If you were given a hundred dollars then your tithe is ten dollars. Look at it as you giving God ten dollar's worth of dimes, or a hundred dimes. *Maybe looking at it in terms of dimes will make it a little easier for you to tithe*.

We have to understand that money is not everything. God is not looking at the money. *God is looking at who He can build a trust relationship with.* The dime is just a medium of exchange to build this trusting relationship. You trusting Him and Him trusting you. The way a good relationship should be. Do you agree with that? I do and I know you do too.

Some people would give away their children before they give away their money. It sounds funny but let them get a little older. They're cute when they are babies but let them become teenagers and you're ready to get rid of them. You'll ship them off to grandma's house quick, fast, and in a hurry. But when you start talking about your hard-earned cash that's different; that's seemingly hard to give up.

To those who don't tithe, what keeps you from giving to God what He is worth? Is it that you think you'll need it or you might not have enough left to pay your bills? Let The Heavenly Father take care of that. Your Father wants to take care of you. Matthew 6:25-26 says,

> **25 "Therefore I say to you, do not worry about your life, what you will eat or what you will drink; nor about your body, what you will put on. Is not life more than food and the body more than clothing? 26 Look at the birds of the air, for they neither sow nor reap nor gather into barns; yet your heavenly Father feeds them. Are you not of more value than they?**

Let me clear up this misconception. Just because you give a tithe doesn't make you a tither. You may give a tithe but are you a tither? To give a tithe implies that even though you may have given it - you don't do it regularly or habitually. That's the reason why so many people, even believers, are in debt. They <u>D</u>o <u>E</u>verything <u>B</u>ut <u>T</u>ithe **(DEBT)**!

The tithe belongs to God. Say it aloud: "The tithe belongs to God".

> **"And all the tithe of the land, *whether* of the seed of the land *or* of the fruit of the tree, *is* the LORD's. It *is* holy to the LORD".**
>
> **Leviticus 27:30**

The tithe is the Lord's. The tithe doesn't belong to the pastor. Even though he/she may be the one who receives it here on earth and there He (Jesus) receives them **(Hebrews 7:8)**. Our High Priest receiving the dime(s) serves as a witness that *He lives*. The phrase *He lives* <u>is in the present</u>

<u>active indicative</u>. *This mean He's alive and right now presently and actively receiving tithes.* So when you hold it back, you're not robbing the pastor. You're not robbing the church. You are robbing God and in the process hurting yourself. When you don't tithe you also allow the devil an inroad into your finances.

I used to be a God-robber, and you probably were one too or still are, but I changed and it wasn't because God took everything from me. God isn't a taker. The Word says in John 10:10 that the devil which is the thief comes to steal, kill and destroy.

> **"The thief does not come except to steal, and to kill, and to destroy. I have come that they may have life, and that they may have [it] more abundantly."**
>
> **John 10:10**

However, once I started to tithe things started to change. Tithing protected the rest of my money. That dime that I give God is a protection over the rest of the 90 percent.

Let me share this with you. I don't necessarily like it when pastors use the term "God is going to get you" as a threat for you to tithe. Love doesn't *get you*. God is love and love isn't out to get or harm you. If my child was a mass murderer (and they aren't) I will still love them. I may not approve of what they do but I will always love them. I would still be there for them and visit them if they allowed me to. God is not trying to throw you away or harm you. What has happened is that the door has been opened allowing the devil to come in and have access into your life. When you don't tithe you place yourself under a curse. You're not cursed, Christ has redeemed you from the curse (Galatians 3:13).

A lot of people will give an offering but not a tithe and that's backwards. It's not okay when you do this. Tithing is mentioned first. That's like going into a restaurant, eating your meal and instead of paying the bill you leave a tip and walk out. **You have to pay what you owe first and then leave the tip.** The devil laughs at you because you're not doing it the right way so he knows it won't work. Don't give him the satisfaction. To **tithe** is The Interstate To Healthy Economics. Reading and studying this book will serve as your wealth GPS. So get moving, you're on the road to financial success and wellbeing.

Chapter 2

Give the Dime Because You Love

Most people tithe out of legalism and not out of love. When you tithe out of legalism you're tithing because you think God is going to get you or He won't bless you if you don't. We're supposed to tithe out of love. Tithe because you love God. I've personally learned to tithe out of love.

When you tithe because you love, you will continue to tithe whether the blessing (return) is manifested immediately, later or not. **But if you tithe just to get something back, if or when it doesn't come fast enough, you'll probably tell yourself, this doesn't work and eventually you will stop tithing.**

When most people stop tithing they stop coming to church. I don't know about you but I want to keep as many people coming to church as possible. Even though you aren't tithing, and I don't condone that, still go to church. God still loves you even when you don't tithe. Also He still wants you to be in church even though you don't think He's worth a dime. But the more you go to church, the more you'll learn and the more you'll get acquainted with Him and His

unconditional love for you. Once you get to know God you'll realize that He loves you and wants the best for you. Knowing a love like that, you'll willfully give Him your money (the dime).

Remember Abraham when he defeated the four kings and brought back all the spoils? (Genesis 14:1, 16-23) Abraham gave God the tithe of the spoils because he loved and honored God. How do I know this? The law wasn't given yet. His tithing preceded the law. So his motive wasn't based out of fear of punishment, expectation of reward or anything like that. Abraham was very rich, so he

16

didn't need a financial blessing as such, he already had wealth (Genesis 13:2). He gave it because he loved God. That's a nominal thought, he loved God. When you give out of love, it will ALWAYS cause you to increase. Receive that!

Also think about Cain and Able and their offering to God. When Cain and Able brought their offering to God it was a sign of worship. I don't see where God gave them instructions as to how and what to bring as an offering to Him because it doesn't say **(and you would have to speculate)**. But I say, they both brought God fruit of their labor as an expression of their appreciation to Him. However I believe Able prepared his gifts to God with more thought, consideration and love than his brother. He offered a more excellent sacrifice than Cain (Hebrews 11:4). And that excellence (love offering) is why I think God received his offering more than his brother's.

All and all, tithing isn't about God collecting dimes or getting money from you. The dime (tithing) is about love, reflection and worship, faithfulness, obedience, promotion and increase, protection, health and The blessing exchange.

17

Chapter 3

The Dime is about Reflection and Worship

"And it shall be, when you come into the land which the LORD your God is giving you as an inheritance, and you possess it and dwell in it, that you shall take some of <u>the first</u> of all the produce of the ground, which you shall bring from your land that the LORD your God is giving you, and put it in a basket and go to the place where the LORD your God chooses to make His name abide. And you shall go to the one who is priest in those days, and say to him, 'I declare today to the LORD your God that I have come to the country which the LORD swore to our fathers to give us.' "Then the priest shall take the basket out of your hand and set it down before the altar of the LORD your God. And you shall answer and say before the LORD your God: 'My father [was] a Syrian, about to perish, and he went down to Egypt and dwelt there, few in number; and there he became a nation, great, mighty, and populous."

Deuteronomy 26:1-15

Tithing begins with an attitude of love for God and a desire to worship and honor Him for what He's given you. When you bring your tithe to the church, you acknowledge that it's not your knowledge, skill, ability, boss, or company that has blessed you. God uses these avenues to deliver the supply to you. He is THE SOURCE. Some of us worship the resources rather than the source. That's why I don't understand how so many people miss church in order to go to work and still don't tithe. **Why?...because you're serving the resource rather than the source.**

In the Old Testament when they gave their tithes and offerings they didn't just drop the money in the bucket (bucket plunking), they worshipped God with it. They held it up and expressed to Him all the great things that He had done for them and how appreciative they were for what He had done.

Reflection is to acknowledge and recognize God for all that He has done.

Worship *or worth-ship* means to show worth of something or somebody through devotion, honor, homage, reverence, and obeisance. **In other words how much is God _worth_ to you.** *Is He _worth_ giving Him a dime off of every one of your dollars?* God is worth so much more than a dime. He is worth everything that you have and more.

Let's look at **"Luke 17:11-18 (NKJV Strong's Bible)**

11 Now it happened as He went to Jerusalem that He passed through the midst of Samaria and Galilee. 12 Then as He entered a certain village, there met Him ten men who were lepers, who stood afar off. 13 And they lifted up their voices and said, "Jesus, Master, have mercy on us!"
14 So when He saw them, He said to them, "Go, show yourselves to the priests." And so it was that as they went, they were cleansed.
15 And one of them, when he saw that he was healed, returned, and with a loud voice glorified God, 16 and fell down on his face at His feet, giving Him thanks. And he was a Samaritan.
17 So Jesus answered and said, "Were there not ten cleansed? But where are the nine? 18 Were there not any found who

returned to give glory to God except this foreigner?"

In verse 17-18, it says "...were there not ten cleansed?

But where are the nine?" In other words, one tenth came

back to give the Father glory/worship. The one-tenth

represents the tithe, the dime. What did that one do? He

came back to give God the glory. He worshipped and

thanked God for what He had done for him. That's what the

dime/the tithe does, it worships and reflects on what God

has done.

> **29 Give unto the Lord the glory due unto his name:bring an offering, and come before him: worship the Lord in the beauty of holiness.**
>
> **1 Chronicles 16:29 (KJV Strong's)**

Your dime(s) express to God how much you appreciate

Him. *Give* God the Glory, He's worthy to be praised!

Chapter 4

Giving the Dime is about Faithfulness

"He who *is* faithful in *what is* least is faithful also in much; and he who is unjust in *what is* least is unjust also in much. Therefore if you have not been faithful in the unrighteous mammon, who will commit to your trust the true *riches?* And if you have not been faithful in what is another man's, who will give you what is your own?

Luke 16:10 –12

If you haven't been faithful over that which is least you're not going to be faithful over the much.   Money isn't everything. God's looking for those he can trust. It's about being faithful. There is an empowerment given to those that can be trusted. You wouldn't put car keys in the hands of a

child because they are immature and not equipped to handle

it. Likewise, you wouldn't trust your money or possessions

to a person who won't put it to good use or value it.

A lot of people are trying to be empowered with what

they can't handle. *They've proven what they can handle by*

proving what they can't handle.

> **"For [the kingdom of heaven is] like a man traveling to a far country, [who] called his own servants and delivered his goods to them. And to one he gave five talents, to another two, and to another one, <u>to each according to his own ability</u>; and immediately he went on a journey."**

> **Matthew 25:14,15**

The parable in Matthew 25 beginning at verse 14

talks about three people who were given some money. One

was given five talents or money; the second was given two;

and, the third was given one talent. At the end, the two that

were given the five and two talents were proven faithful

because they went and made interest off of the money they were given. They invested it and got a return.

> **"His lord said to him, 'Well [done], good and faithful servant; you were faithful over a few things, I will make you ruler over many things. Enter into the joy of your lord.'"**
>
> **Matthew 25:21**

The person that was given the one talent didn't get any interest on his money but instead buried it. The Bible called him *unprofitable* and that he should be cast into outer darkness where there is weeping and gnashing of teeth.

> **"Then he who had received the one talent came and said, 'Lord, I knew you to be a hard man, reaping where you have not sown, and gathering where you have not scattered seed. And I was afraid, and went and hid your talent in the ground. Look, [there] you have [what is] yours. But his lord answered and said to him, 'You wicked and lazy servant, you knew that I reap where I have not sown, and gather where I have not scattered seed. So you ought to have deposited my money with the bankers, and at my coming I would have received back my own with interest. So take the talent from him, and give [it] to him who has ten talents. 'For to everyone who has, more will be given, and he will have abundance; but from him who does not have, even what**

he has will be taken away. And cast the unprofitable servant into the outer darkness. There will be weeping and gnashing of teeth.'" Matthew 25:24-30

Let me say this, I don't believe you'll go to hell if you don't tithe. However the devil will make it seem like hell financially speaking. The devil will devour what's not covered by the dime. I just wanted to clear that up.

Have you ever noticed that the people who are tempted not to tithe the most are the ones with the least. The servants' lord gave the three according to their faithfulness or ability. The man knew who he could trust just like God knows who He can trust with His goods. So if you don't have that much it's because you can't handle it yet.

Notice I said YET. **You determine that you can be faithful in the much when you are faithful with the least.** It's left up to you; what are you going to do about that? I sense those dimes coming out of those pockets and purses.

The Word says that if you're not faithful over that which is least who will give to you that which is much. God will give you more when you show you're trustworthy. If you can't be trusted with a dime what makes you think I'll give you ten thousand dollars. ***The dime is just a test.*** *This is only a test, I had to say that.* It is just to prove if you're ready to go to the next level. And a lot of people are proving that they are not ready to go to the next level by holding on to the dime.

When you are not faithful over another man's belongings, who will commit to you your own. If I loan you my car and my car comes back trashed you won't get it again. However, most people will be more careful with someone else's belongings than they are with their own. So if you're not faithful over another man's belonging than who will trust you enough to give you your own.

Give that dime faithfully and watch how you abound with the blessing (Proverbs 28:20).

Chapter 5

Giving the Dime is about Obedience

"If you are willing and obedient, you shall eat the good of the land,"

Isaiah 1:19

Bring all the tithes into the storehouse so that there may be meat in my house. It's about obeying God and doing what He has required of you.

A lot of people aren't obedient in this area because they put their circumstances before God. You can't just be willing, you have to also be obedient. The New Living Translation says it this way.

"If you will only obey me and let me help you, then you will have plenty to eat."

NLT

This is an obedience to the faith. What does that mean? Tithing is faith personified. When you tithe you are saying that I have faith in what God said He would do when I tithe. God wants to help you and you need some help! God can't help you if you won't let him help you. God will not do

more than you allow Him to. You will always have your needs met if you're obedient to the faith. The word said,

when you obey you will HAVE, let's stop right there. You will **have;** I don't know about you but I want to have, don't you? Have what? Plenty to eat! You will never be without. That sounds like El Shaddai, the God of more than enough.

> **"Bring all the tithes into the storehouse, That there may be food in My house, And try Me now in this," Says the LORD of hosts, If I will not open for you the windows of heaven and pour out for you [such] blessing that [there will] not [be room] enough [to receive it]."**
>
> **Malachi 3:10**

28

You have to be obedient to this faith process and bring all the tithes into the store house. <u>If you are obedient you won't even have enough room to receive all that God has for you.</u> He's talking about insights, concepts, ideas and witty inventions. Some of you are millionaires already; God has given you witty ideas that you are just sitting on and letting other people capitalize off of your talent, or letting it go to waste because you are lazy. I'm not trying to be mean by saying that but it's the truth.

> **"Another parable He put forth to them, saying: 'The kingdom of heaven is like a mustard seed, which a man took and sowed in his field, which indeed is the [least of all the seeds]; but [when it is grown it is greater] than the herbs and becomes a tree, so that the birds of the air come and nest in its branches."**
>
> **Matthew 13:31, 32**

The least thing that you give in God's system, He will make great. If you release **the mustard seed** it becomes greater than all the trees and herbs in the earth. The birds can lodge there. Other things and people will benefit because of your obedience to the small things. Don't show up in God's record book as not giving anything. When you don't tithe you're hindering your own manifestation of finances **(the window of heaven's blessings)** but you open a window of devastation for any and everything else to happen.

> **"Those who sow in tears shall reap in joy. He who continually goes forth weeping, Bearing seed for sowing, Shall doubtless come again with rejoicing, Bringing his sheaves [with him]."**
>
> **Psalms 126:5,6**

You may be crying all the way to church with your tithe in your hand, thinking "I can't afford this." But let me tell you, you can't afford not to tithe. God knows you really need it, you know you really need it. But the Bible says **when you sow in tears you will reap in joy**. Can you remember times when you sowed in tears and were so glad that you did? You came back with increase because of your obedience to the faith. I have several testimonies of partners who have obeyed and some miraculous things happened. One I can remember, a young lady in our church who needed some clothes for work and money for food but she gave and doors were opened. She got to work and the employer told everyone they could dress down for the week or month, I don't recall exactly. So she didn't have to purchase new clothes. Isn't that like God? Also, she was treated to lunch, look at God! Hallelujah!

If you don't tithe and give an offering you are allowing the enemy to hinder your financial increase **(the windows of heaven's blessing)**. You can confess that every need is met all you want, but you can't be disobedient to this faith process and circumvent God's way of doing things. People always want to use the excuse that the pastor(s) just want their/your money. Can I tell you something that might shock you? All Walmart, Target, Nordstrom's, Dillard's, Nike, Adidas etc. want is your money. Conversely, when they're faced with financial difficulties they run to the church for a bail out. How do you think the church gets the money to help you out when you need it? They get it from givers (tithers and offerers) like us.

Let me cancel this misnomer. The church is not a savings and loan. The purpose of tithing and giving offerings is not for you to come and make withdrawals whenever you want or have a need. There was a couple in our church who was buying their first home but they didn't have the initial down payment or closing costs, I don't really remember which. However, they asked to meet with me, when I did, guess what they wanted? You got it. All the tithes they had given to the church. I bet you're saying what? What is right! Mind you, they weren't tithers, they would give a tithe here and there. Let me just say, tithers are those who tithe consistently. The tithes and offerings they gave, given that they both were professionals, equaled up to something like a couple of thousand dollars I believe. Now guess what I did with their request. I hope you don't think I'm insensitive but I laughed. I told them we used that money for kingdom business. Some people feel that whenever they have a need the church is supposed to dish out money to them. Needless to say, they went away upset at the denied request. They got the house and a few years later lost it. Okay, let's get back into the subject at hand.

Tithing isn't about giving God what's left it's giving God what's right. After you pay your mortgage, your utility bills, put new rims on your car, get your weave in and then you say these two dollars are all I have leftover to give God, that isn't right. You're supposed to give God the tenth first.

Partial obedience equals full disobedience. Remember, tithing isn't giving God what's left it's giving God what's right.

A lot of people are unfortunately doing this. They finish paying all their bills and everything else, then they give Him what's left over. **In this crumbling economy we better start investing in the kingdom of God because the world's system is failing.** God's system is the only system that will stand. When billion dollar corporations start letting thousands of employees go and stores that have been around for years and years start shutting down - you know that you need to do something. The only sure thing to do is to get on God's system. Stop giving God what's left and give him what's right.

Chapter 6

The Dime is for Promotion and Increase

"Bring all the tithes into the storehouse,
That there may be food in My house, And
try Me now in this," Says the LORD of
hosts, If I will not open for you the windows
of heaven and pour out for you [such]
blessing that [there will] not [be room]
enough [to receive it]."

Malachi 3:10

There will not be enough room to receive it. That's

promotion – that's increase. When you tithe, there will be so much that there won't be enough room to receive all that

God has for you. That's overflow.

> **"Give, and it will be given to you: good measure, pressed down, shaken together, and running over will be put into your bosom. For with the same measure that you use, it will be measured back to you."**

> **Luke 6:38**

You're going to have to tell people to stop giving to

you because you have so much. You can't beat God's

giving. There was a song we used to sing in church which

said, ***"You can't beat God giving no matter how hard you***

try. The more you give the more He'll give to you. Just

keep on giving you'll find His word is true, you can't beat

God giving no matter how hard you try." If you give to

Him He will always outdo your giving. You may not get it

back that day but you will get it back with increase.

Tithing isn't a faith talk it's a faith walk. Tithing takes

action. Do it because you want to show Him how much you

love and believe Him! It's just not about what you say it's what you believe/do. I can't confess that all my needs are met when I'm robbing God. All your needs are met in the spirit realm but you won't have it manifested.

Just because you're due for a promotion on your job doesn't mean you will automatically get it. However, every time I was due for a promotion I received mine. Why? Because tithing and giving ensured my promotion and increase. **When you tithe and give you will always go up.**

> **"A faithful man will abound with blessings, but he who hastens to be rich will not go unpunished."**
>
> **Proverbs 28:20**

If you're not faithful in the least you will not be promoted. Let me share with you something I learned from Bishop TD Jakes.

The number ten is a number of wholeness and completion. It's the first level of your giving. It's the least. When you tithe faithfully you are telling God you are ready to go to the next level. **Ten is as high as you can count because eleven is one on the next level.** For example, when you start counting 1,2,3,4,5,6,7,8,9,10 it starts again on the next level 11,12,13,14,15,16,17,18,19,20 Then again 21,22 and so on. **So when you don't tithe you tell God to keep you right there on that same level because you're not ready to go to the next level.** Once you can start giving the dime off of every dollar or the dollar off of every ten or the ten off of every hundred you let God know that you're ready to go to the next level.

When you tithe you say to God I have gone as high as I can go on this level. Now promotion and increase is inevitable.

Stop telling God to take you to the next level if you haven't proven yourself at your current level. You say, God I need some more money. You've already proven what you would do with it. If He gives you more money that means you'll ignore Him even more. You may not even come to church any more. You get your new car and ride pass the church waving "Hey Pastor". God's not going to give you any more money because He knows what you're going to do with it. That statement isn't all together the truth, because God would give you more money but you wouldn't be able to handle it. More money would just magnify what you're doing now. If you know what I mean.

Promotion comes when you have maximized productivity at your present level. If you can't give God a dollar off of the ten dollars you can't go to the next level because you're not maximizing what He's blessed you with already. You've gotten in over your head in bills and now you want to make excuses why you don't tithe and God wants to help you. Excuses are the support system of the uncommitted, the mediocre, the status quo and the lazy. So tithe and let Him help you. God loves you so much He will even help you with troubles of your own making. **If you want promotion and increase tithe.** Now that you're tithing, you're ready to go to the next level.

Chapter 7

The Dime is for Protection

"And I will rebuke the devourer for your sakes, So that he will not destroy the fruit of your ground, Nor shall the vine fail to bear fruit for you in the field," Says the LORD of hosts;"

Malachi 3:11

Most people that read this verse don't pay attention to what they're reading or saying. This verse says, I will rebuke the **_devourer_** for your sake. But when most read this verse, it's like it says devour and not devourer. There's a big difference. **One is the result and the other is the cause.** God goes right to the source, right to the root of the thing that's causing the problem. He deals with surface things via

the root. Just like Jesus cursed the fig tree. He wanted the

tree gone and He cursed the tree and it **dried _up_ from the**

root. Approximately twenty-four hours later the tree was

totally dried up. It had begun to dry up at the root. The

devourer is a person, I believe it's the devil (i.e. the enemy,

satan). If you continue to read verse 11 it says, "So that _**he**_

will not destroy the fruit of your ground,..." Did you get that?

**He will not destroy** the fruit of your ground. It's not for

God's sake that the devourer is being rebuked it's for your

sake. The word rebuked mean **"stop it now."**

The tithe represents the whole of your money. The

dime represents every dollar that you make. When you tithe

He protects all the rest after you tithe and give your offering.

God can't protect what you haven't sanctified.

> **"For if the firstfruit [be] holy, the lump [is] also**
> **[holy]: and if the root [be] holy, so [are] the**
> **branches."**
>
> **Romans 11:16**

If you make $50,000 a year, a month, a day, receive that! However, if you tithe on half of it you leave the other part exposed to the devil. At that point he can come in and wreak havoc on the unprotected portion. Bills you thought were gone and forgotten might reappear. That school loan you haven't paid will come in the mail. You graduated twenty years ago and you got a bill in the mail for school with interest.

When you tithe you simply tell God all of my finances are under YOUR control and protection. When people question you about tithing, they say things like *"you tithe and give all your money to that man or to that church"*. Your response should be *"And you don't tithe? What's the matter with you?"* Look at them like they're the strange one – but in actuality you are the strange one. Look at what they called the only leper out of the ten that came back to give God glory. Luke 17:18 (King James)

18 There are not found that returned to give glory to God, save this _stranger_.

What if the pastor or the church is/was mishandling the money, you did what you were supposed to. That person would have to be accountable for not doing what he or she was supposed to. So don't make excuses as to why you don't give. Remember what I said earlier, excuses are the support system of the mediocre, the lazy, the uncommitted and the status quo.

You're not supposed to have to work two and three jobs to get by. Years ago before I started tithing, I was working two jobs. I went from one job being on my feet all day then working as a barber cutting hair which required me to be on my feet for at least another five hours. Once I got a hold of tithing over thirty years ago, I quit that second job because I wanted to prove God's Word in my life. Guess what? I didn't

have to work two jobs anymore. One of two things or both

could be why you are still working two jobs. One is you're

living above your means or two you're not tithing correctly.

> **"Honour the LORD with thy substance, and with the firstfruits of all thine increase: So shall thy barns be filled with plenty, and thy presses shall burst out with new wine."**
>
> **Proverbs 3:9**

If God is not LORD of all, He's not Lord at all. If you

don't sanctify the whole with the tithe, He isn't Lord at all in

that area of your life.

> **"For if the firstfruit [be] holy, the lump [is] also [holy]: and if the root [be] holy, so [are] the branches."**
>
> **Romans 11:16**

Put your financial well-being in a safe place, in God's

protection!

Chapter 8

The Dime is for Health

"And I will rebuke the devourer for your sakes, **So that he will not destroy the fruit of your ground, [Nor shall the (vine) fail to bear fruit] for you in the field," Says the LORD of hosts;"**

Malachi 3:11

"Your wife [shall be] like [a fruitful vine] in the very heart of your house, Your children like olive plants all around your table."

Psalms 128:3

Nor should your vine cast her fruit before her time in the field, says the lord of hosts. Your children shall be like fruitful vines. God will protect the health of your children. He'll also protect your health. The woman is like the vine and the children are like the olive berries. Tithing will protect against miscarriages, premature deaths, etc.

The devil is the devourer. He comes to steal, kill and destroy (St John 10:10). What does the devourer come to steal, kill and destroy? The answer is *everything*, which includes your health. There is an in road to your body for Satan when you don't tithe. He can make you sick where you can't work or you don't have health insurance. So your body and your finances will be destroyed. He will come in and create things with your health to zap your money. If I sanctify the whole of my money by giving my tithes the rest of it will be protected.

Don't blame God or the devil when you get sick and you don't have insurance. Some people think that sickness comes to make you strong. Some people think that sickness comes so that God can get your attention or teach you a lesson. They say, my momma died from this or that because God wanted another flower in his bouquet. Do you think God would want you (the family) to suffer? Get real, how stupid is that? We've been promoting this lie in church

for years. God didn't do that! It was the devil, the enemy.

He comes to steal, kill and destroy. Does it sound like I'm

passionate about this? Yes I am! I'm tired of people lying on

my Father.

> **"Now He was teaching in one of the synagogues on the Sabbath. And behold, there was a woman who had a spirit of infirmity eighteen years, and was bent over and could in no way raise [herself] up. But when Jesus saw her, He called [her] to[Him] and said to her, "Woman, you are loosed from your infirmity." And He laid [His] hands on her, and immediately she was made straight, and glorified God."**

> **Luke13:10**

> **"So ought not this woman, being a daughter of Abraham, <u>whom Satan has bound</u>--think of it--for eighteen years, be loosed from this bond on the Sabbath?"**

> **Luke   13:16**

If sickness was a part of trying to get someone

humbled He would have left the woman in this parable sick.

Rebuke every illness that comes up even the common cold. The Word says, **"Whom Satan has bound,"** he attacks your physical body. But you can keep him away by tithing, also I might add, by eating right.

I can hear some of you say, so I have to pay God to heal me. No I'm not say that. I can't believe you asked that question knowing how much healthcare cost? If He did charge, you wouldn't be able to afford His plan anyway. Also it would be a drastic reduction in what you're paying now I'm quite sure. You wouldn't have to renew it every year either. Besides, the doctor and the benefits are out of this world.

> **"In all your ways acknowledge Him, and He shall direct your paths. It will be health to your flesh, and strength to your bones.**
>
> **Proverbs 3:6,8**

In all your ways include your finances too. There's a study that says, those that tithe and give offerings are healthier than those that don't do it. So do it and you'll feel better.

Chapter 9

The Blessing Exchange

"For this Melchizedek, king of Salem, priest of the Most High God, who met Abraham returning from the slaughter of the kings and blessed him, to whom also Abraham gave a tenth part of all, first being translated "king of righteousness," and then also king of Salem, meaning "king of peace," but he whose genealogy is not derived from them received tithes from Abraham and blessed him who had the promises. Now beyond all contradiction the lesser is blessed by the better."

Hebrews 7:1-2, 6-7

In the Old Testament it appears that people tithed and then they were blessed. But in reality they were blessed first and then they tithed. Most of the time the word blessed is referred to in terms of material wealth. That's not incorrect but it is incomplete. Blessed or the blessing means to empower to prosper. This empowerment extends beyond material wealth. Abraham became very rich because of his wife Sarah (Genesis 12:16; 13:2). Sarah is a type of *grace* (Galatians 4:21-31). Grace was the initial reason he was made very rich. After the slaughter of the Kings, Abraham became wealthier from gathering in the spoils. He gave a tithe of the spoils to Melchizedek *(a picture of Jesus)* who in turned blessed him.

When you give your tithe you're just continuing the cycle of the blessing. Let me explain. **You can't tithe except you are empowered** *(blessed)* **to prosper first.** You can only tithe or give your ten percent *(the dime)* after you get some money. Be it through a job, a gift, an inheritance or an insurance claim etc. Tithing is reinvesting a part of what you were given in the first place by the one who blessed you! You're blessed first and then you tithe and you're blessed again and you tithe again, etc. Hopefully you realized when I said by the one who blessed you, I wasn't talking about your boss or job. It is/was your Heavenly Father. He is the source of the blessing and your job is one of the re-sources He uses. Let me share with you something else. The word **tithe** in the Hebrew is the word *Ma'aser.* Now *Ma'aser* has the Hebrew word *aser/asar* which means *prosper/rich.* The tithe has the *rich* in it already. You should tithe because God **has already** made you rich.

The less is blessed of the better! You are the less and God is the better if you didn't know it. When God blesses you become rich, that's called cause and effect. Is it all about the money? **No!** *Money is simply a means to an end.* It gets us what we want. **You don't really want the money you just want the stuff money can buy.**

Money is to be used in exchange for things. Have you noticed that your U.S. dollar bill has Federal Reserve Note printed on the top of it? Also, printed in smaller letters on the left front of the bill is the phrase "THIS NOTE IS LEGAL TENDER FOR ALL DEBTS, PUBLIC AND PRIVATE," which means it can be used in exchange for goods and services. It's not to be served or worshipped. But people are going after money like its God. However, to some it maybe a god (i.e. small g god). Get a grip, **"In God We Trust"** not money. Even that phrase is printed on the back of the money you're working so hard to get. The dollar bill itself tells you where to put your confidence and trust, in God! You can't serve them both. It's one or the other. Matthew 6:24 says it like this,

> **24 "No one can serve two masters; for either he will hate the one and love the other, or else he will be loyal to the one and despise the other. You cannot serve God and mammon.**

All I'm saying is this, if you trust God to bless you with the things you need, you wouldn't have to work so hard. Tithe **(i.e. make the exchange)** and trust God to provide for you. Honestly the money we use from day to day isn't worth the paper its printed on. This world's system of economics isn't geared towards prospering you. This system is in place to keep you borrowing and broke. Give to it and it <u>might</u> give you a return but it isn't promised. God's system of economics makes you the lender and not the borrower. When you give to it **(i.e. make the exchange)**, blessings WILL BE multiplied to you.

Some of you might be saying, I've never tithed before what's going to happen if I you do? One thing I can tell you,

God will never be in debt to anyone. Let me also share with you, the Lord is able to give you more than what you give Him.

> **9 And Amaziah said to the man of God, But what shall we do for the hundred talents which I have given to the army of Israel? And the man of God answered, <u>The Lord is able to give thee much more than this.</u>**
>
> **2 Chronicles 25:9 (KJV Strong's)**

Release the tithe (dime) even though you don't see or

know how it's going to work. What I can tell you, God has

more than enough waiting for you when you do. He has the

good measure, pressed down, shaken together and running

over that you won't have room enough to receive kind of

blessing for you. Get a revelation of that and it will be easy

to make the exchange.

Pray this with me for revelation; *Father I thank you*

that the eyes of my understanding are open and I KNOW

what is the hope of your calling concerning the RICHES of

the glory of Your INHERITANCE in me and also what is the

exceeding greatness of Your power toward me because I

*BELIEVE in this **blessing exchange principle**. And*

because I believe, when I release my tithes and offerings it

will be given back to me, in a good measure, pressed down,

shaken together and running over. I expect supernatural

involvement in every area of my life especially my finances.

I say, my mind is open to receive new concepts, insights,

ideas and witty inventions that will make me a financial blessing to the kingdom of God and everyone I come in contact with. The windows of heavens blessing remain open over my head and no man can shut it in Jesus name!

Act on, believe and confess this and the floodgates of the blessing will start to open up more for you. It will come upon you and overtake you because of your obedience to this faith process (Deuteronomy 28:1-2; Luke 6:38). When it comes and overtakes you, keep that blessing cycle going by continuing to tithe like we discussed earlier in this chapter. Also be open to Holy Spirit's promptings to give. He will make you a distribution center of the blessing to others. You're blessed to be a blessing. You'll be a blessing going somewhere to happen.

Lastly, don't mistake this blessing exchange as an opportunity to buy everything you've ever wanted. Things like the latest and greatest iProducts; iPhone, iPad and iPod and can't say at the end of the day iTithe. ***Say aloud,* I'm blessed therefore iTithe.**

Chapter 10

A Dime Worth of Testimonies

The Bible says that a faithful man abounds with blessings (Proverbs 28:20). It's all about being faithful. Do you recall the stewards in the book of Matthew whose master divided out talents to them? He wasn't talking about tap dancing or singing. He was talking about money. Some translations actually use the word money. He gave one man five talents or five pieces of money, the next he gave two talents, and the other he gave one. Which one had the problem? It was the man who had the one talent. And it appears the one who doesn't have that much has a problem with giving. They feel, since I don't have much, why should I have to give? I say to them, if you don't give you cant expect to receive. You can't keep it to yourself and think it's going to multiply mysteriously without investing it. That doesn't even happen in the world system.

In order to make money you'll have to give money or invest it. You'll **never** be a millionaire or billionaire, like John D. Rockefeller, Bill Gates, Donald Trump or Charles Williams if you keep your money in your pocket. You can put your name there when you give your tithes and offerings regularly. You may ask, why did you put your name in that list? I'm speaking those things that be not as though they are (Romans 4:17) and you can too.

I was reading a book called the Millionaire Next Door; most of those guys who were millionaires and billionaires in that book tithed. They tithed because they understood the principle of giving the dime (ten percent). That's the tithing principle. Rockefeller tithed. Trump tithed. They all tithe. In other words, they gave at least ten percent away to churches or non-profit organizations. Let me tell you what I learned about John D. Rockefeller. According to Forbes in 2006 John Rockefeller was/is still one of the richest people in the world. They said if his assets and net worth was put together at that time in 2006 he would be worth 336 billion. Bill Gates assets and net worth as of November 2014 was 82 billion. Bill Gates I believe learned from Rockefeller how to tithe, give to and start charity foundations. Rockefeller's mother taught him at an early age to tithe. When he received his first earnings as a working child, his mother showed him what he needed to give to the Lord as a tithe. And from that time forward he tithed all the money he earned. This is what he said and I quote, ***"I did, and from that week until this day I have tithed every dollar God has entrusted to me. And I want to say, if I had not tithed the first dollar I made, I would not have tithed the first million dollars I made. Tell your readers to train their children to tithe, and they will grow up to be faithful stewards of the Lord."***

Now the ones who need more money don't tithe. In turn, they stay in the position they're in, not having enough. But the millionaires who tithed had money beyond their wildest dreams because they did what was right by tithing.

You must have a clear understanding of why and how to tithe, because if you don't, Satan will come and snatch what you think you know out of your heart.

> **"When anyone hears the word of the kingdom, and <u>does not understand it</u>, then the wicked one comes and snatches away what was sown in his heart."**
>
> **Matthew 13:19**

Putting an arbitrary amount on the tithe line of your church's envelope doesn't mean that's your tithe. That's just a number you put on the tithe line to deceive the finance ministry. God can read. He can see and add. He knows how much you are supposed to tithe. So don't be foolish.

Many ask, do I tithe off the gross or the net? This is my response to that question. You can tithe what you want to, gross or net.   You may not understand what that question means, tithe off the gross or net.   Or why I said what I said.   Let me explain.   Tithing off the net means, after all the taxes are taken out, all the insurance payments and everything else comes out then you give ten percent off of what's left.   Tithing off the gross is when you give the ten

percent before all the deductions are taken out.   Abraham gave tithes of all the spoils and besides God said to bring **all** the tithe... and that means to me, the gross.

"Bring all the tithes..."

Malachi 3:10

"...and he gave him tithes of all (gross)."

Genesis 14:20

Now I have a question for you. Do you want a net return or a gross return? A net or gross manifestation of the blessing? Of course you want a gross return.   But I don't make that much money.   My tithe wouldn't matter.   It wouldn't be a significant amount anyways.   I'm reminded when Jesus wanted to feed the multitude in St John 6. He asked His disciple Philip "Where shall we buy bread that these may eat?" "But He did that **to test** him, for He Himself knew what He would do." Philip answered Him, "two hundred pennies worth of bread is not enough for them...." Then Andrew said, "There is a lad here who has five barley loaves and **two small fish**, but what are they among so many?" (St John 6:5-9). He did that to **test** him. That sounds like Malachi 3:10, "Bring all the tithes into the storehouse, that there may be food in My house, And **try** Me now in this, says the LORD of hosts, "If I will not open for you the windows of heaven And pour out for you such blessing that there will not be room enough to receive it." The word **test** in Greek in John 6 and the word **try** in Hebrew in Malachi 3 are companion words meaning the same thing. The five barley loaves and **two small fish**, resembles the tithe. In comparison, the two small fish and the tithe appears insignificant to what it's up against: inflation, bills, needs and wants. But and this is a BIG but, when you place your little in the hands of Jesus it becomes much. It will feed thousands and pay bills and you will have money left over to do whatever else you need to get done.

So never be ashamed of your tithe/dime no matter how small

it is. If your tithe is an actual dollar, give that dollar.

"...it is accepted according to what one has, and not according to what he does not have."
II Corinthians 8:12

Don't be ashamed. God honors that dollar tithe just

as He would honor a person who tithe a thousand dollars

because they did it in obedience to the faith. The woman

who had only the mite (a small gift) gave more than them all

because she gave all she had.

If 10% isn't too much to receive; why is it too much to

give? When you're in the store and a salesperson says

they'll give you 10% off your purchase, why do you reply, is

that all. You can at least give me 20% off. Why is 10% so

much at church and it's not a lot at the store. Do you want

me to tell you why? **It's a trick of the enemy.** He doesn't want you to tithe so that he can have access to your finances. Come on, it's just a dime for every dollar you receive. Is that so much to give? No it isn't! Will you continue to let that dime rob you of all the provision (exchange) God has for you? I'm confident that you won't.

There was a gentleman in my congregation who told me this story. He came to the service this particular Sunday and all he had to his name was a dime. Holy Spirit was urging him to give me the dime, but he was too embarrassed. He said to himself, Pastor is worth more than a dime. Finally after obeying Holy Spirit's prompting and giving me the dime he soon found out that it was the beginning to his blessing exchange.

He testified that he didn't not like to work, however, soon after he landed a job or should I say career, God blessed him to be a partner in the company that he is employed by.

This is the power of the dime. Now let your dime do the same for you!

ABOUT THE AUTHOR

Dr. Charles K. Williams is a native Washingtonian who accepted Jesus Christ as his Lord and Savior when he was 16 years old. At the age of 27, he accepted his five-fold ministry call in the area of pastor/teacher. After working eight years at the Department of Transportation & pastoring full time for 5 years, he resigned from his management position in 1997 to give himself wholly to his call. As a result of his obedience to the voice of God, God began to reveal His word even more in the area of faith & finances and The Standard of Living Ministries was birthed.

In July 2000, he received his Doctorate Degree of Divinity. Not only has he served as the Washington, DC Area Director for the Fellowship of Inner City Word of Faith Ministries (FICWFM) founded by Dr. Frederick K.C. Price, he served as PTA president at Kramer Middle School in Washington, DC for two years.

He is known for serving and spreading hope in the community. He's committed to helping and giving to those in need as well. Because Dr. Charles' teaching style of ministering has been described as simplistic and practical so that even children can apply it to their everyday life; he has incorporated that effective teaching style into his writing, thus his first book *"God Ain't Worth a Dime?"*

Once you began reading this book, you will not want to put it down until you've finished.